Turning Points
in the lives of
Great Men and Women of the Bible

By
Matt Hennecke

ISBN 13: 978-1-58427-394-3
ISBN 10: 1-58427-394-1

Guardian of Truth Foundation
CEI Bookstore
220 S. Marion St., Athens, AL 35611
1-855-49-BOOKS or 1-855-492-6657
www.CEIbooks.com

truth
BOOKS

```
┌─────────────────────────────────────┐
│                                       │
│         A NOTE TO TEACHERS            │
│   To assist you in teaching these lessons │
│        notes may be available at      │
│          the following website:       │
│                                       │
│         www.biblemaps.com             │
│                                       │
└─────────────────────────────────────┘
```

A NOTE TO TEACHERS
To assist you in teaching these lessons
notes may be available at
the following website:

www.biblemaps.com

CONTENTS

LESSON 1: Abraham   5

LESSON 2: Joseph   9

LESSON 3: Moses   13

LESSON 4: Joshua   17

LESSON 5: Ruth   21

LESSON 6: David   25

LESSON 7: Elijah   29

LESSON 8: Jonah   33

LESSON 9: Manasseh   37

LESSON 10: Daniel   41

LESSON 11: Esther   45

LESSON 12: Turning Point in Our Lives   49

"turning point" - noun

1. *a point at which a decisive change takes place.*
2. *a point at which something changes direction, especially a high or low point in one's life.*
3. *a moment when the course of events is changed; i.e. the turning point of one's life.*

BIBLE TURNING POINTS

ABRAHAM

When God called Abraham out of Ur of Chaldees (Gen.15:7) he had a choice to make – whether to answer the call of God or to refuse. In choosing to leave his home and venture into the unknown, Abraham's life was forever changed. We are not told much about Abraham's early life – or of the events that led him to accept God's call – but his faith was strong enough that he packed up his family and his belongings and began a journey that first took him to Haran and finally led him to settle in Canaan (Gen. 12 4-5; Heb. 11:8-10). While Abraham's faith was sufficient to get him moving, there were events in his life which revealed his faith was, perhaps, not as strong as God would have it be.

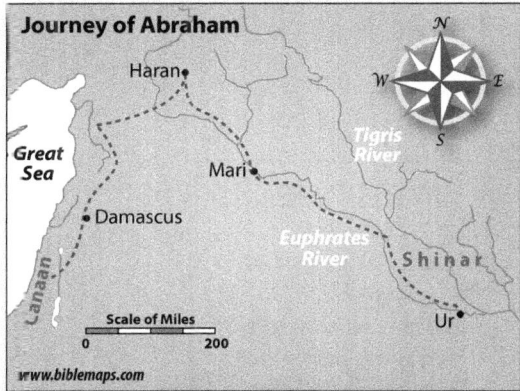

Journey of Abraham

Haran

Great Sea

Damascus

Mari

Canaan

Scale of Miles
0   200

www.biblemaps.com

Tigris River

Euphrates River

Shinar

Ur

N
W E
S

1. Read Genesis 12:1-4. What promise did God make to Abraham that implied he'd have children? How old was he at the time?

2. Read Genesis 12:10-20. What did Abraham conspire to do with Sarai? Did this demonstrate a lack of faith?

3. Read Genesis 16:1-2. What did Abraham agree to with Sarai to "help" God fulfill the promise He'd made in Genesis 12? Did this indicate a lack of faith by Abraham?

4. Read Genesis 17:1-8. What did God again promise? How old was Abraham at this time?

"I am God Almighty."
- Genesis 17:1

IN HIS TIME
In His time, in His time,
He makes all things beautiful
In His time.
Lord please show me every day
As You're teaching me Your way,
That You do just what You say
In Your time.

- Words and Music by Diane Ball

5. Read Genesis 17:15-21. What was Abraham's response to God's promise of a son by Sarai? What might this say about Abraham's faith?

6. Read Genesis 20:1-11. What deception did Abraham conceive to save his life from Abimelech, King of Gerar? What might this say about Abraham's faith in God's power to fulfill His promises?

ABIMELECH

TURNING POINT

Read Genesis 22:1-19. The events recorded in Chapter 22 represent a "turning point" in the life of Abraham. While he had shown moments of faith to this point, the *almost* sacrifice of Isaac demonstrated a faith that is strong enough to obey God whatever the price.

7. How was it possible for Abraham to follow God's commands to sacrifice Isaac?

8. How did Abraham reconcile the seeming contradiction between what God had promised to him and what God had commanded of him?

God promised me a great nation through Isaac.	HOW?	God has commanded me to sacrifice Isaac.
THE PROMISE		THE COMMAND

9. How could a loving God ask Abraham to sacrifice his only son – the son of promise?

Mt. Moriah

What is the significance of the place where Isaac was to be sacrificed?

WE LOVE OUR IDOLS

In one of her books Elizabeth Elliot makes the point that the process of Christian growth is one in which God breaks the idols of our life one by one by one. Oh, how painful it is because by definition, we love our idols. We protect them because they give us strength and hope and meaning. Here's the tricky part. Most of our idols are perfectly good things. That thing I was holding on to so tightly wasn't anything bad or evil or wrong. It was something good that had become too important to me. Pause to consider this sentence:

An idol is anything good that becomes too important to you.

We tend to associate idols with those heathen statues made of gold, silver, wood or stone. And if that's all an idol is, we're in the clear because we don't bow down before those weird statues and offer pig blood or chicken entrails. Why would we do something like that? But an idol doesn't need to be a statue. An idol can be anything good – our children, for instance – or our fame, our athletic prowess, our reputation, our money, our home, our position, our education, our cars, the people we know, the degrees we earned, the money we made, the deals we closed, the classes we taught, the friends we cultivated in high places, the buildings we built, the organizations we managed, the budgets we balanced, the books we wrote, the songs we sang, the records we made, the trips we took, the portfolios we built, the fortunes we amassed, our name in the lights, all those things that make us feel comfortable and safe and give us status in the world.

Source: Dr. Ray Pritchard in an online sermon entitled *What is Your Isaac?* at Keep Believing Ministries.

What Do You Most Love?

INSTRUCTIONS: In box 1, indicate the person in this life that is most precious to you. In box 2 indicate the possession that you most prize in this life.

1	*The most precious person to me:*
2	*My most prized possession:*

JOSEPH

The story of Joseph is one of the most beautiful found in the pages of God's word. From an early age Joseph seems to have possessed a strong faith that carried him through many difficult times. His faith, unlike Abraham in our last lesson, seemed unshakeable even at an early age. Perhaps it was the dreams he had when young (Gen. 37:5-11) that convinced him that, despite trials and setbacks, he was destined for greatness. Of course, there were likely times when Joseph felt despair, but the Bible is silent about such moments. Instead, the Bible reveals the trials in Joseph's life before the "turning point" when he was elevated to rule with Pharaoh in Egypt. The stages of Joseph's life, it has been suggested, can be studied by considering the clothes he wore as he grew from a youth to the second most powerful ruler in Egypt.

A Coat of Many Colors - Genesis 37:1-11, 18-24

1. What was the first setback in the life of Joseph? How old was he at this turning point? Is there any symbolic significance to the coat he wore?

2. Read Genesis 37:25-28. How did Joseph's life become even worse?

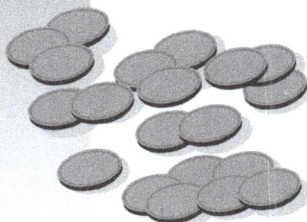

20 shekels of silver ▬▬▬▬▬

A shekel is a unit of weight, roughly equal to 10.5 grams. In 2010 a gram of silver was worth just under 50 cents. Some sources suggest, however, that silver was much more valuable in biblical times. A shekel of silver may have been worth as much as $30 U.S. dollars.

The Coat of a Servant - Genesis 39:1-19
As Potiphar's servant, Joseph – despite his youth – made the best of the situation.

3. How was Potiphar's household blessed by Joseph's presence?

4. What other biblical characters can you think of who thrived even while in captivity? To what do you attribute the ability of God's people to do well even in adversity?

The Coat of Suffering - Genesis 39:19-23
While in prison suffering unjustly Joseph wore prison clothes (inferred from the fact he changed his clothes when he later went before Pharaoh. (See Genesis 41:14.)

5. How did Joseph behave as he dealt with this "turning point" in his life?

6. What was Joseph's "secret" to thriving even in the face of such adversity?

The Coat of Deliverance - Genesis 41:1-8,14-16
While in prison Joseph demonstrated the power given him by God to interpret dreams. Later, this ability would bring him in new garments into the presence of Pharaoh.

7. What happened to the two fellow prisoners whose dreams Joseph interpreted?

8. For how long did Joseph suffer in prison?

9. Who or what was responsible for Joseph's deliverance?

TURNING POINT

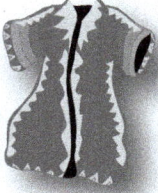

The Coat of Royalty - Genesis 41:33-43
After all that had beset Joseph in his life he at last attains a place of royalty, second only to Pharaoh.

10. Relate the events in Joseph's life (illustrated below) to a similar "journey" of Christ and of Christians. (See Phil. 2:5-11; Rom. 6:3-7.)

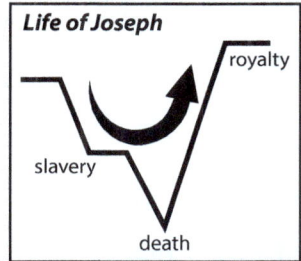

Life of Joseph

royalty

slavery

death

11. What lessons are there for us in the life of Joseph?

12. How is the story of Joseph an encouragement to men and women of faith today?

ALL THINGS WORK TOGETHER FOR GOOD
TO THOSE WHO LOVE GOD
- Romans 8:28

13. Were the events in the life of Joseph part of some plan of God? See Genesis 45:4-8.

14. List below some events in the Bible that while seeming to be bad initially, ultimately worked out for the good.

Thought Question

What events in your own life seemed bad initially but have since turned out for good?

Consider it all joy, my brethren, when you encounter various trials,
knowing that the testing of your faith produces endurance.
And let endurance have its perfect result,
so that you may be perfect and complete, lacking in nothing.
- James 1:2-4

BIBLE TURNING POINTS

D. L. Moody once said this of Moses: *"Moses spent 40 years in Pharaoh's court thinking he was somebody; 40 years in a Midian desert learning he was nobody; and 40 years showing what God can do with somebody who found out he was nobody."*

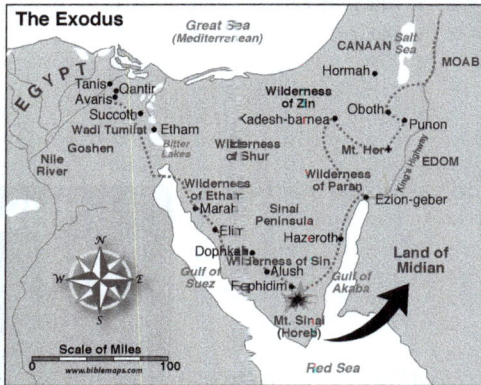

There can be no doubt Moses is one of the greatest figures of the Old Testament: with God's help he delivered the Lord's people out of Egyptian bondage, led them for 40 years in the wilderness, and is also credited with having written the first five books of the Bible (the Pentateuch). Despite all of his accomplishments, Moses was certain he was *not* the man for the job. His résumé was certainly not impressive: he was old; he was hot-headed; he was a fugitive; and he was full of excuses.

1. Read Exodus 2:11-25. What injustice did Moses observe that led to his fleeing to the land of Midian? Did Moses know at this point in his life that he would deliver God's people?

2. What injustice did Moses see in the land of Midian he felt compelled to rectify? What was the result?

3. What do these two events reveal about Moses' character?

The 5 Excuses of Moses

4. Read Exodus 3:1-15. What was the first excuse (v. 11) Moses gave when God called him for the task of delivering His people?

5. What might Moses have thought worked against his being called for this important task?

6. What was Moses' second excuse (v. 13) and what was God's response to his question (vv.14-15)?

7. What is meant by God's assertion that He is the I AM" (v. 14)?

YHWH

YHWH typically pronounced *Yahweh* (translated as *Jehovah*) is a name that conveys God's being. God is the only self-existent and self-sufficient being in the universe. Only God has life in and of Himself. It further conveys the idea of "timeless existence."

8. Read Exodus 4:1-17. What was the third excuse (v. 1) Moses attempted in his efforts to convince God to find someone else?

9. What was Moses' fourth excuse (v. 10) and what was God's response? Reconcile Moses' excuse with what Stephen said about him in Acts 7:22.

10. What final excuse – a plea really – did Moses employ (v. 13)? What was God's reaction and solution?

What symbolism, if any, may be suggested by God appearing in a burning bush?

TURNING POINT

11. Out of excuses, Moses began his mission of deliverance, yet still seemed a bit tentative. See Ex. 5:22; 6:12, 30. When was Moses' "turning point" – that is, when did his complaining and insisting he wasn't right for the job turn to confidence and strong leadership?

12. What lessons can we learn from Moses' initial resistance to God's call and the leadership he later demonstrated? List 2 lessons for us below:

LESSON 1

LESSON 2

"I'm good enough at making excuses that I don't have to be good at anything else!"

Argue for your limitations and sure enough they're yours!
- Richard Bach

MOSES AND US

Imagine for a moment that you had been called by God to deliver those held in captivity. What would be your response? Would you willingly give yourself to the Lord to fulfill His purpose?

Interestingly, we have been called to deliver those in captivity – captivity to sin. In Romans 8:28 we read that *"God causes all things to work together for good to those who love God, to those who are called according to His **purpose**."* God's purpose is for us to *"go into all the world and preach the gospel"* (Mark 16:15-16), but like Moses, we often use the same excuses he used. Excuse making is sometimes referred to in psychological journals as "self handicapping." In other words, people purposefully "create handicaps" for ourselves which allow them to refuse to do what needs doing while at the same time preserving their self image.

An excuse is worse than a lie, for an excuse is a lie, guarded.
- Alexander Pope

LIE

Lest we condemn Moses too much, we must first consider ourselves. Who among us, knowing the will of God for our lives, has not lingered too long before accepting His call?

Question for Discussion
What do you think are the 2-3 most common excuses made by Christians to excuse themselves from sharing the good news of the gospel with a friend or acquaintance?

Success comes in CANS not in CAN'Ts.

SUCCESS

BIBLE TURNING POINTS

JOSHUA

There is no Old Testament figure more unwavering in his fidelity to God than Joshua. From the time we are first introduced to him as he led God's people in battle against Amalek (Ex. 17:9), to those final, beautiful words near the end of his life when he declares *"...as for me and my house, we will serve the LORD"* (Josh. 24:15), Joshua proved himself a leader of amazing faith and conviction. Unlike many biblical characters whose turning points came when their fragile faith became strong, Joshua's faith seems to have been strong from the beginning. His turning point – the subject

of this lesson – came when he was chosen to replace Moses as the leader of God's people. How did he do it? How did he prepare for the awesome task of leading an unruly people? If you have ever felt overwhelmed with responsibility (rearing children; being a single parent; caring for an ailing loved one; being an elder, preacher, or teacher), if you ever felt yourself incapable of filling some "big shoes" or taking on a big role in godly service, then Joshua's turning point story is for you.

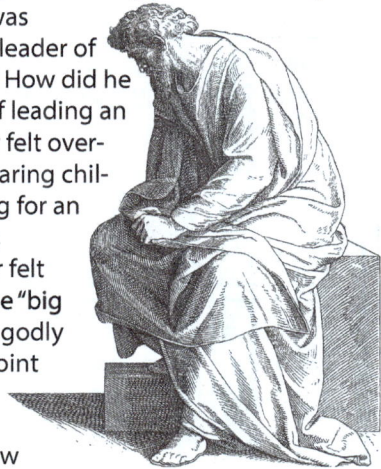

1. Read Joshua 1:1-11. Given how strongly the LORD encourages Joshua what might we infer he was feeling about replacing Moses?

2. What is notable about Joshua's response to God's call (vv. 10-11)? How does it compare to Moses' response when he was called to lead God's people (Ex. 3)? How do you account for the different responses to God's call?

5 Things that Threatened to Overwhelm Joshua

1. Read Deuteronomy 31:7-8. What great things had Moses done during the time he led the people? How might this have given Joshua pause about assuming the role of leader?

2. What was the destination of God's people? What stood in the way of that goal (Deut. 7:1)?

Nations of Canaan
(Before the Conquest)

Great Sea
Sidonians (Phoenicians)
Girgashites
Bashan (Kingdom of Og)
Sea of Chinnereth
Canaanites
Perizzites
Transjordan
Jordan River
Hivites
Ammonites
Sihon (Amorites)
Jericho
Jebus
Jebusites
Mt. Nebo
Hittites
Salt Sea
Kenites
Moabites
Amalekites
Edomites

© 2012 MANNA Bible Maps
www.biblemaps.com

3. What were the people's expectations about possessing a land of their own?

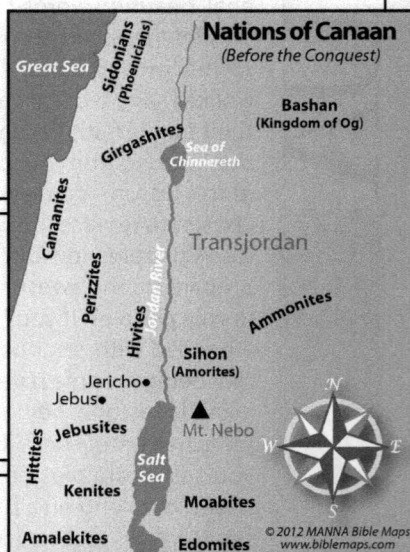

4. What prophecy – certainly known to Joshua – was made about the people? See Deuteronomy 31:14-17.

5. What does Deuteronomy 4:22-24 say about God and His expectations? What had kept Moses from entering the promised land?

ISRAEL

TURNING POINT

With a staggering responsibility before him, Joshua, without apparent hesitation, assumed the role Moses had held for over 40 years. The key to his success at this "turning point" in his life is revealed in Joshua 1:8.

This book of the law shall not depart from your mouth, but you shall meditate on it day and night, so that you may be careful to do according to all that is written in it; for then you will make your way prosperous, and then you will have success.
- Joshua 1:8

3. Consider the verse above and indicate below what you find notable about its instruction.

4. What does it mean to "meditate" on something? Is meditating different than reading? How does one go about meditating on the Word?

5. Did Joshua successfully follow the Lord's instruction based on the results of his leadership? See Joshua 24:31.

BE STRONG AND COURAGEOUS

A child had to walk each evening past a dark, spooky house. Some adult friends tried to give him courage. One handed him a good-luck charm to ward off the ghosts. Another installed a light at a particularly dark corner near the house. A third took a more spiritual approach, saying, "Don't be afraid. Trust God and be brave!" It was good advice, but not much help. Then one friend said with compassion, "I know what it's like to be afraid. I'll walk with you past the house." Instantly the child's fears were gone.

This was what God did for Joshua. Joshua faced the task of leading a group of desert nomads against the trained armies of established kingdoms. That would be enough to make even the bravest man afraid.

The Israelites were concluding 40 years in the wilderness due to fear. What they saw as impossible kept them from doing what God had wanted. They could have entered the promised land years earlier, except for fear.

But now was the time and the place and God did more than give Joshua a battle plan or a pep talk. He reassured him, saying, "I will be with you wherever you go. Fear not."

Jesus said these very same words as he sent the eleven disciples out to all the nations. He did not say they would not be afraid. He said, "I shall be with you always, even to the end of the world" (Matt. 28:20).

God does not promise He will not lead us into fearful situations. He may call us to serve Him in distant lands or God may ask us to stand up for Him right here in this town. In either case, we may be quite afraid. Sometimes the biggest fears are right at home. But just like Joshua, we can do it because God also has given us the solution for the fear: He has given us Himself.

Source: From an online sermon entitled "Strong and Courageous: A Sermon Based on Joshua Chapter 1" written by Tim Henry on Yahoo Contributor Network.

BE STRONG AND COURAGEOUS

Be strong and courageous,
* You hosts of the Lord!*
Rise up for the battle,
* And gird on your swords!*

The land of His promise
* Is yours now by right,*
Take all He has given;
* Go forth to the fight.*

Be stong and courageous,
* Consider His law;*
Regard it with reverence;
* Perform it with awe.*

Be careful to follow all
* God has decreed,*
For then He will bless you,
* And you will succeed.*

- Glenda B. Schales

Final Question: Has there ever been a time when you – despite overwhelming circumstances – demonstrated strength and courage in doing what needed doing? Who or what gave you strength?

BIBLE TURNING POINTS

5 LESSON

Within the pages of the Old Testament are many beautiful and inspiring stories but none is more beautiful or more inspiring than the story of Ruth. In its four short chapters is revealed a human tapestry of rich colors and interwoven threads which speak not only of the suffering of life, but of a God who makes everything beautiful in His time.

While the story is amazing in its own right, it is also an allegory of God's love for each one of us who, broken by life, are in desperate need of a kinsman-redeemer. The story of Ruth, then, is our story. It has been left to us so we might learn of the power of love, sacrifice, and commitment. It is a story divinely preserved through the centuries to touch us, teach us, and point us to Christ. Please read the entire book of Ruth in preparation for this lesson. It's a beautiful story and well worth your time to read it.

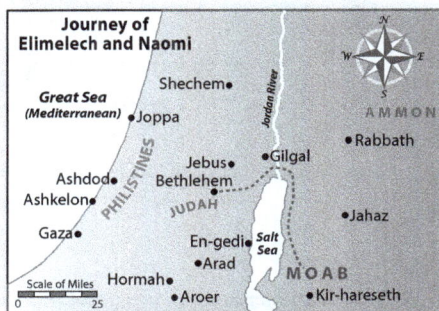

1. What drove Elimelech, Naomi and their two sons to the land of Moab (1:1-2)?

2. What calamity befell Naomi? What did her two sons do? What happened to Naomi's sons 10 years later?

3. What decision did Naomi make and what did she tell her two daughters-in-law to do?

TURNING POINT 1

The first "turning point" in Ruth's life comes early in the narrative. Naomi insists Ruth return to her homeland rather than return with her to Jerusalem, but Ruth declines, choosing instead to accompany Naomi. Her beautiful words of fidelity to Naomi have echoed down through the centuries:

Turning point of CHOICE

> *Do not urge me to leave you or turn back from following you;*
> *For where you go, I will go, and where you lodge, I will lodge.*
> *Your people shall be my people, and your God, my God.*
> *Where you die, I will die, and there I will be buried.*
> *Thus may the Lord do to me, and worse,*
> *If anything but death parts you and me.*
> *- Ruth 1:16-17*

4. Ruth's decision has seemingly guaranteed a life full of suffering. List 5 challenges Ruth *had* faced or would *now* face by her decision:

RUTH'S 5 CHALLENGES

1
Ruth 1:5

2
Ruth 2:11

3
Ruth 2:11

4
Ruth 2:11

5
Ruth 4:13

5. How might Ruth's vow to Naomi have actually helped her deal with her own losses? What lessons are there in Ruth's selfless action for us?

TURNING POINT 2

The second "turning point" in Ruth's life occurs in chapters 2-4 when her circumstances suddenly change and all of the challenges she was facing are swept aside. This "turning point" in her circumstances results in her becoming the wife of an influential and worthy man named Boaz.

Turning point of CIRCUMSTANCE

6. Who was behind the dramatic change in Ruth's circumstances?

7. What stirred Boaz to show such kindness and mercy to Ruth (Ruth 2:10-12)? Is it possible his generosity was inspired by Ruth's generosity?

8. Was there some master plan at work which caused the famine, sent Elimelech and Naomi to Moab, and brought Ruth back to live in Bethlehem to meet and marry Boaz? See Romans 8:28.

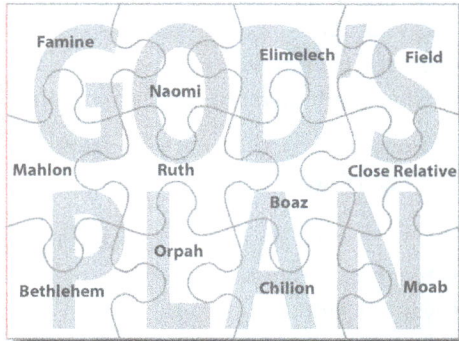

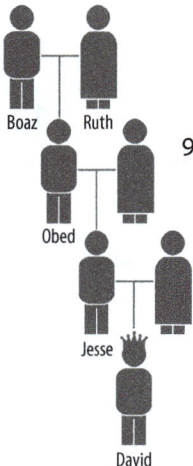

9. Does the story of Ruth and Boaz foreshadow events that later transpire in the New Testament involving Christ and His bride, the church? What significance, if any, is there in the idea of a "kinsman-redeemer"? See Hebrews 4:15.

PAY IT FORWARD

In the 2000 movie *Pay It Forward*, a 12-year-old boy's social studies project – to change the world by doing three good deeds for people, who in turn do three good deeds for others, and so on – becomes a national movement. The concept is lovely, but is it really possible to spread kindness?

A new study by researchers at the University of California, San Diego and Harvard University suggests it is. Their work, published in the Proceedings of the National Academy of Sciences, provides laboratory evidence that kind behavior spreads. Those who benefit from kindness tend to find it contagious and "pay it forward" by helping others.

The authors, James Fowler, an associate professor of political science at UC San Diego, and Nicholas Christakis, a Harvard

The Domino Effect of Kindness

sociology professor, showed that when one person engaged in random acts of kindness to help others, the recipients were more likely to engage in kind acts to others. The domino effect continued as more people were swept up in the tide of kindness and cooperation, according to the researchers. In short, Fowler said: "You don't go back to being your 'old selfish self.'"

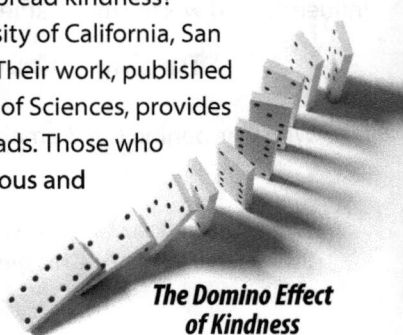

Source: Pay It Forward: Research Suggests Generosity is Contagious by Christina Hernandez Sherwood, March 11, 2010

While it is clear Boaz was a good man in his own right, his kindness to Ruth was in part prompted by the great kindness she had shown to Naomi (2:10-12). Given the kindness shown to us by God in sending His Son to die for us, what should be our response?

UP FOR A CHALLENGE? ━━━━━━━━
This week engage in three random acts of kindness for someone you don't know, and be prepared to share the effect being kind had on you and them. Jot down what kind acts you did below:

1.

2.

3.

BIBLE TURNING POINTS

The Bible is a rich source of encouragement. Within its pages are numerous events and stories that provide insight into the human condition. These events, selected by the Holy Spirit for inclusion in the Holy Word, reveal the mind of God and show His care and concern for mankind. Sometimes, however, we may miss important lessons because we become preoccupied with the main thread of a story. If we dig a bit deeper, if we look a bit closer, there are often other threads, other lessons for our encouragement. One such event is the story of a young man – a boy really – who clashed with a giant of a man and emerged victorious. We all know the story of David and Goliath, but we may have missed other lessons it offers because our attention is drawn to the main event. If we look closer, what we discover is that in reality there were five giants with which David fought. These same five giants often confront and taunt us. Let's revisit the events recorded in 1 Samuel 17, for they represent a "turning point" in the life of a shepherd boy who would one day be a King. Read 1 Samuel 17.

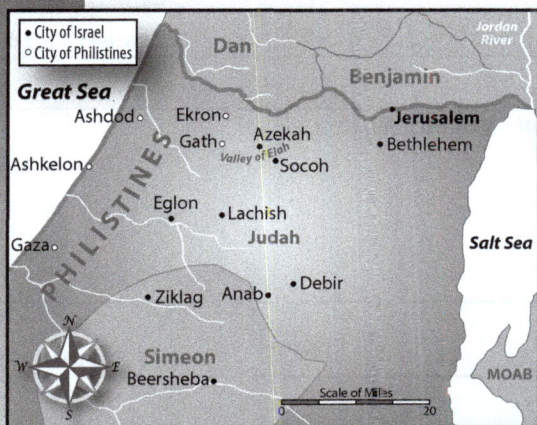

1. Circle the location of the clash between David and Goliath.

2. How tall was Goliath?

3. How much did his armor weigh?

4. How much did the head of his spear weigh?

5. What about Saul's height may have made him a good choice to fight Goliath?

- City of Israel
- City of Philistines

Dan

Jordan River

Benjamin

Great Sea

Ashdod

Ekron

Gath

Azekah

Valley of Elah

Jerusalem

Bethlehem

Ashkelon

Socoh

Eglon

Lachish

Gaza

Judah

Salt Sea

Debir

Ziklag

Anab

Simeon

Beersheba

Scale of Miles

0   20

MOAB

PHILISTINES

Goliath
While the Hebrew text of the Bible and certain editions of the Septuagint give Goliath's height as "six cubits and a span," Josephus (*Antiquities* 6.171) and a Dead Sea Scroll fragment both give his height as "four cubits and a span."

1 Samuel 9:2

David and the 5 Giants

INSTRUCTIONS: A careful reading of 1 Samuel 17 reveals David had many "giant" obstacles to overcome. What obstacles stood in his way to achieving victory, and how might these "giants" manifest themselves in our lives today?

1 Samuel 17:28-29

Giant of....

How might this giant manifest itself in our lives?

1 Samuel 17:33, 42

Giant of....

How might this giant manifest itself in our lives?

1 Samuel 17:38-39

Giant of....

How might this giant manifest itself in our lives?

1 Samuel 17:24

Giant of....

How might this giant manifest itself in our lives?

1 Samuel 17:41, 43-44; 1 Peter 5:8

Giant of....

How will this giant manifest himself in our lives?

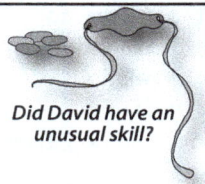

GIANT
5

Did David have an unusual skill?

6. What three rewards were offered by the King to the one who would go out and fight Goliath and prevail against him? See 1 Sam. 17:25.

TURNING POINT

After the defeat of Goliath, David's life was never the same. From obscurity he rose to a preeminent position in Israel. 1 Samuel 18:5 says, *"David went out wherever Saul sent him, and prospered; and Saul set him over the men of war. And it was pleasing in the sight of all the people...."*

A King made a promise to reward whomever would defeat the enemy. Does that sound familiar to a child of God?

7. How is the coming of Christ fore-shadowed in David's victory over Goliath?

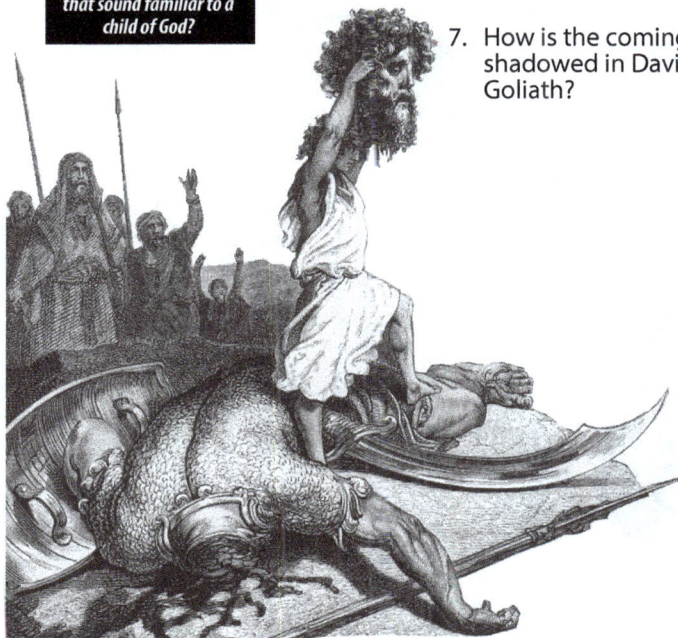

Turning Points - 27

LETTING GO OF OUR "BAGGAGE"

Without exception, all of us carry "baggage" – those fears, apprehensions, and behaviors which are defined by our earliest experiences. Our relationships with parents, siblings, relatives, and others early in our lives – both positive and negative – shape many of our future behaviors.

When we enter a friendship or relationship, we are implicitly agreeing to take on and deal with the other person's unique "baggage." The success or failure of most relationships is determined by the gradual discovery of the contents of the other's "baggage" and then discovering within ourselves the ability, willingness, and desire to help carry what is there.

In the spiritual realm, it is interesting to note that when we come to Christ, we find in Him someone who will accept us despite our "baggage" and will help us turn loose of those burdens and be freed of their weight. Jesus said in Matthew 11:28, *"Come to Me, all who are weary and heavy-laden, and I will give you rest. Take My yoke upon you and learn from Me, for I am gentle and humble in heart, and you will find rest for your souls."*

Additionally, fellow Christians are charged with the responsibility of helping to carry each others burdens – that is, the "baggage" we cannot bear alone and which threaten to exhaust us. Paul said in Galatians 6:2, *"Bear one another's burdens, and thereby fulfill the law of Christ."*

The challenge for each of us is to refrain from hiding in our baggage – being stymied by our fears – but instead to leave our baggage behind in the care of the Baggage Keeper and go forward into the spiritual battles knowing full well that the LORD will see us through to victory.   - Matt Hennecke

Question for Discussion
Why was Saul afraid to confront Goliath while David was unafraid?

ELIJAH

BIBLE TURNING POINTS

In the Bible record the prophet Elijah appeared suddenly without fanfare or introduction and pronounced a great drought in Israel because of the sins of the people under the leadership of evil King Ahab (1 Kings 16:30; 17:1). Then, after three and half years without rain, events came to a head on Mt. Carmel when Elijah taunted Baal, whom the people had been serving, and through God performed several miracles which convinced the people that "the LORD, He is God." The prophets of Baal were seized and slaughtered by the brook Kishon and rain finally fell on the parched land.

In the aftermath of Elijah's great victory, Jezebel, Ahab's wife, sent a messenger to Elijah, threatening to kill him the next day and Elijah we are told "was afraid and arose and ran for his life." Please read 1 Kings 19.

Elijah's name means "Jehovah is my strength."

© 2012 MANNA Bible Maps

1. The Jews highly esteemed Elijah, but what does James 5:17 tell us about him?

2. How many miles did Elijah run to escape Jezebel? _____ miles

3. Why do you think Elijah chose Mt. Horeb as a hiding place?

4. Why do you think Elijah fled – especially when he had seen the power of God so recently exhibited? For how long did he journey?

"WHAT ARE YOU DOING HERE?"

Instructions: The question posed by God to Elijah as he hid in the cave on Mt. Horeb is a bit ambiguous. What word was the LORD emphasizing as He asked that question? Consider the different possible meanings below:

*"What are **YOU** doing here?* – of all possible people

5. Perhaps the point of God's question was that Elijah of all people should have known better than to flee. Why should Elijah have known better?

*"What are you **DOING** here?* – of all possible actions

6. Perhaps the point of God's question was that Elijah's actions were inconsistent with a man of God. How were Elijah's actions inconsistent with a man of God?

*"What are you doing **HERE**?* – of all possible places

7. Perhaps the point of God's question was that of all the places Elijah might have been, being in a cave was not where he should be. Why is hiding not really an option for a man (or woman) of God?

Is this the "cleft of the rock" in which Moses had seen the glory of God pass by (Ex. 33:19-23)?

TURNING POINT

The LORD showed remarkable compassion on Elijah as he fled from the threat of Jezebel. As he sits in a cold, dark cave on Mt. Horeb, the LORD provides a demonstration that is both powerful and puzzling. Re-read 1 Kings 19:11-14 and be ready to explain what is meant by the demonstration.

8. What three powerful demonstrations of God's power did Elijah observe? Why is it said God was *not* in those manifestations?

9. What is the final manifestation of God (1 Kings 19:13)? Was God in that final manifestation? If He was, why does Elijah seem unchanged? Think about it and provide an explanation of the point God was making from these events:

10. What was the "turning point" in Elijah that got him out of hiding and seemingly restored his confidence?

ANOTHER MOUNTAIN TOP EVENT

11. In an earlier lesson we studied Moses and in this lesson we've considered Elijah. While these two great men of the Bible were separated by some 500 - 600 years, they do appear together later in the biblical record. In what biblical event do we see these two men together and what are we to make of their reappearance?

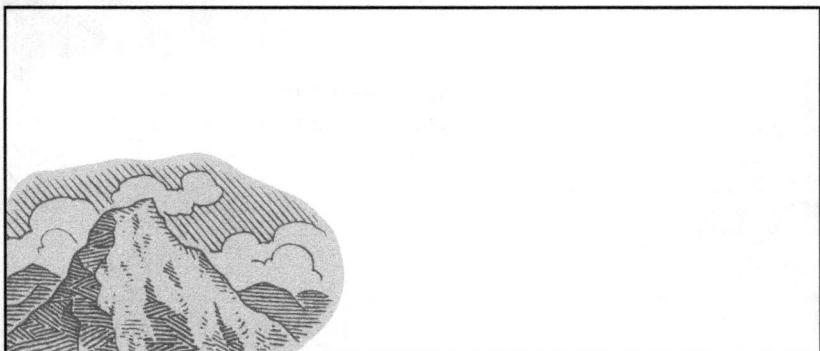

WHAT ARE **YOU** DOING HERE?

Have you ever wondered why God created man? Think about it. After existing eternally, why did God decide to create man? Did the creation of man fulfill some need God had? We are told in Scripture that God is love (1 John 4:8). Would it be correct to assume God *needed* an object of His love? We may never find an answer to that question, but the fact is God did create man and that raises yet another question: For what purpose was man created? Or put another way, what are **YOU** doing here? Indicate below what you believe to be man's purpose for existing:

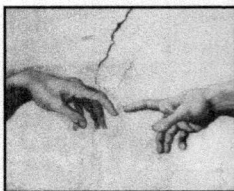

JONAH

BIBLE TURNING POINTS

Several years ago my brother and I decided to try some class 5 whitewater rafting on the Arkansas River through the Royal Gorge in Colorado. The guide gave the six of us in the raft some specific instructions: "There's a part of the river that's very dangerous – a woman drowned last week on this part of the river." In a serious voice he continued, "The water drops over a 15-foot waterfall and the force causes the water to form a 'knuckle' that rides forcefully back on itself. When we go over the falls paddle with all you've got and if we get caught in the knuckle listen for my voice and then climb for your lives to the high end of the raft to prevent it from tipping." What did we do? We paid close attention! Sure enough, when we went over the waterfall we were caught in that knuckle and our raft spun around and then suddenly began to tip, threatening to dump us into the raging water. "Now!!!" yelled our guide, and we all scrambled for our lives to the top of the raft. At the last possible second, our combined weight forced the raft down and we were spared being tossed into the turbulent water.

Because we followed our guide's advice and because he had learned from the mistakes and successes of prior trips, we were saved. To put it another way, *we learned from those who went before us.* That is a good principle to remember in life: It's always less painful to learn from the mistakes of others. Experience is a good teacher, even when it's someone else's experience!

This lesson will focus on the experiences of a prophet named Jonah which will provide us some crucial lessons and maybe even save our spiritual lives.

1. We are briefly introduced to the prophet, Jonah, *before* the book that bears his name. Where is that reference, and what prophecy does Jonah make?

2. Was Jonah's prophecy good or bad news? Do you think he was pleased about delivering that prophecy? Why?

"...the Lord appointed a great fish to swallow Jonah...."
- Jonah 1:17

3. Read the book of Jonah. Some have argued the story of Jonah is a fable and not to be taken literally. Is the book a fable or is it a factual account of what happened to Jonah?

4. Trace the journey of Jonah on the map. Which direction did God want Jonah to go? Which direction did he go?

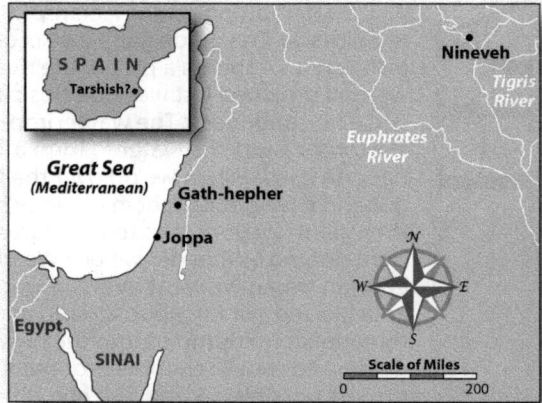

5. How do you account for Jonah's apparent willing response to preach in 2 Kings 14:25, and his unwilling response to preach in Jonah 1:1-3?

SPAIN
Tarshish?

Nineveh

Tigris River

Euphrates River

Great Sea (Mediterranean)

Gath-hepher

Joppa

Egypt

SINAI

Scale of Miles
0   200

6. As you consider events of Chapter 1, how many times did Jonah go "down"? (Consider verses 3, 15, and 17 as you fill in the spaces below.)

Jonah went....

Every step away from the will of God is a downward step.

1 "Down" to _____(v.3)

2 "Down" into _____(v.3)

Is Jonah's downward path in some ways similar to Christ's? See Matt. 12:38-40.

3 "Down" into _____(v.15)

4 "Down" into _____(v.17)

TURNING POINT

Jonah's turning point comes in the belly of that great fish as he prays to God. His prayer reveals he is no longer fleeing *from* God, but instead is ready to flee *to* God. In describing Jonah's change of heart, R.T. Kendall wrote: *"The belly of a fish is not a happy place to live, but it is a good place to learn."*

7. The key to Jonah's salvation – indeed the message of the book of Jonah and of the entire Bible – is found in Jonah 2:9. What is that simple, yet powerful message?

8. Did Jonah really understand what he said as he concluded his prayer to the LORD in Chapter 2? What was his attitude as he preached to the Ninevites? Had he made the "turn" in his understanding? See Jon. 4:1-3.

9. What sin does it seem Jonah committed even as he preached to the Ninevites? See James 2:1-10. In what ways might we be guilty of judging the people of the world as unworthy of salvation?

Thought Question

Did Jonah ever really repent, or did he do God's bidding merely because he was forced to do so? Be ready to share your observations and make your case in class.

NOT WORTHY OF SALVATION

Nineveh was the capital of Assyria, the most powerful empire in the world in that day. The Assyrians had a reputation for cruelty that is hard for us to fathom. Their specialty was brutality of a gross and disgusting kind. When their armies captured a city or a country, unspeakable atrocities would occur: things like skinning people alive, decapitation, mutilation, ripping out tongues, making a pyramid of human heads, piercing the chin with a rope, and forcing prisoners to live in kennels like dogs. Ancient records from Assyria boast of this kind of cruelty as a badge of courage and power.

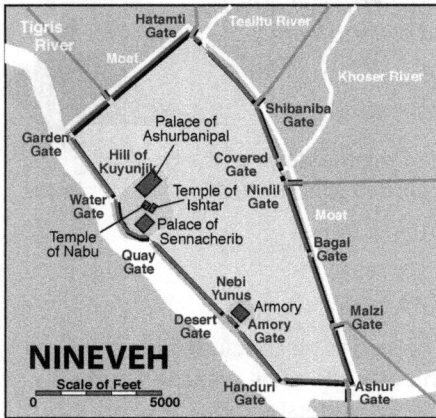

The Assyrians had no use for the Jews, and the Jews hated the Assyrians: hated them for their bloodthirsty cruelty, hated them for their idolatry, hated them for their arrogance. For a Jewish man to be told by God to go preach to Nineveh was repugnant. As far as Jonah was concerned, Nineveh could go straight to hell. "Go ahead, Lord. Push the button. Open the trapdoor. Let 'em fall straight down into the pit." That's how Jonah felt about Nineveh. For Jonah the Ninevites were not worthy of salvation. Jonah had already judged them and deemed them not worthy of his care or attention.

Source: Online sermon by Dr. Ray Pritchard entitled "We're Just Like Jonah – Jonah 1," Keep Believing Ministries.

To Whom Would You Give Greater Attention?

In each of the six pairings below indicate with a checkmark in box A or C the individual in the pairing to whom you would be inclined to give more attention or show more concern. Put a checkmark in box B if neither.

	A	B	C	
1. Physically attractive person				Physically unattractive person
2. An older adult				A younger adult
3. A very poor person				A very wealthy person
4. A Democrat				A Republican
5. Someone of a different race				Someone of the same race
6. A highly educated person				A poorly educated person

BIBLE TURNING POINTS

As we journey through life we come in contact with all kinds of people. Some have a positive impact on us, while others leave us with a bitter taste in our mouths. It's kind of like the sign hanging in a country inn: *"Everyone blesses this place: some by staying, some by leaving."* Isn't that true? There are some people we *hate* to see leave and others we struggle not to *hate*. We tend to remember those who left a positive impact – perhaps because of their kindness and encouragement or their bright outlook on life. Others, sadly, we remember because they made our days darker by their scowling, cynical dispositions. The negative ones we avoid, and if they are especially negative – leaving destruction in their wake with lies and wickedness – we write them off. We conclude they are too far gone to ever change. But, how do we *know* a person won't change? Who put us in the role of their judge and jury? Do we ever have the right to conclude that someone is so bad that he will never put aside his evil ways and repent? In this lesson we will have our eyes opened to the amazing grace of God who can and will forgive even the most despicable of people if they will simply repent of their ways and humbly seek His forgiveness. Read 2 Kings 21 to prepare for this lesson.

1. What influences or factors in Manasseh's life would lead one to believe he would turn out to be a good king?

*eryone blesses this place.
by staying, some by leaving.*

GOOD AND EVIL INFLUENCES

2. What influenced him to lead a life of evil rather than good?

3. Do you think Manasseh's father was in some ways responsible for the evil path Manasseh took? Is Proverbs 22:6 *always* true or is it *generally* true?

4. Complete the résumé below, indicating based on the verses listed all the things King Manasseh accomplished during his 55 year reign in Judah.

MANASSEH'S RÉSUMÉ OF EVIL

WORK EXPERIENCE

King of Israel   687 – 642 B.C.
CoRegent with King Hezekiah   697 – 687 B.C.

ACCOMPLISHMENTS

21:3 _____

21:4 _____

21:5 _____

21:6 _____

21:7 _____

21:9 _____

21:16 _____

21:20-22 _____

Baal

Baal is mentioned widely in the Old Testament as the primary pagan idol of the Phoenicians, often associated with the heathen goddess Ashtaroth. Unfortunately, to their eventual bitter regret, the Israelites became deeply involved in the cult of the Baals. The evil "worship" included perverted sexual behavior and even sacrificing their infants in fire. It wasn't just misguided – it was outright wickedness. - Wayne Blank

5. What, in your mind, was the most heinous sin committed by King Manasseh?

What does it mean he "made his son pass through the fire" (21:6)?

6. How bad was King Manasseh in comparison to other evil kings who had ruled God's people? See vv. 9, 11.

7. In His anger, what did the LORD plan for Judah and what analogy did He use in describing the calamity that would befall Judah?

TURNING POINT

Read 2 Chronicles 33:10-20. What events occurred that led to Manasseh's "turning point"? How do you account for the LORD forgiving and restoring Manasseh as King? What lessons are we to learn from Manasseh's change?

8. List below the lessons can we learn from the life of Manasseh.

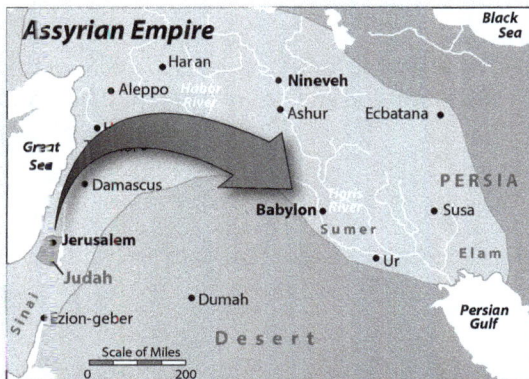

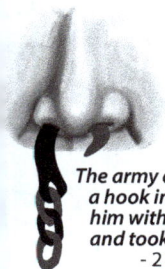

The army commanders put a hook in his nose, bound him with bronze shackles and took him to Babylon.
- 2 Chronicles 33:11

Assyrian Empire

Black Sea
Haran
Aleppo
Nineveh
Ashur
Ecbatana
Great Sea
PERSIA
Damascus
Babylon
Susa
Sumer
Jerusalem
Ur
Elam
Judah
Dumah
Persian Gulf
Sinai
Ezion-geber
Desert
Scale of Miles
0   200

THE RIGHTEOUS AND THE WICKED

INSTRUCTIONS: Create two lists below. The first list should be the names of living or *recently* deceased individuals who you believe are or were examples or models of righteousness. The second list should include the names of living or *recently* deceased individuals who you believe epitomize wickedness.

Examples of Righteousness

1
2
3

Examples of Wickedness

1
2
3

Now consider both lists and answer the following questions:

9. What is your attitude toward those on the righteous list? In other words, what do you *wish* or *desire* for them?

10. What is your attitude toward those on the wicked list? What do you *wish* or *desire* for them?

11. What do you believe to be God's wish or desire for those listed above? Is your attitude and desire different than God's? Why?

Think About

12. Does God love those on both lists equally? Do we? Should we?

BIBLE TURNING POINTS

DANIEL

AND HIS THREE FRIENDS

LESSON 10

The book of Daniel tells a story of several young people who were taken captive to Babylon because of the sin of God's people in Judah. It is likely Daniel was descended from a royal family and may have been a prince since history reveals the prominent were typically taken captive by the Babylonians after they conquered a land (Dan. 1:3). Best estimates are Daniel was about 15 years old when he was abducted from his home and that by the end of the book he was about 70 years old. Unlike many of the other great men and women we have studied, Daniel's "turning point" comes right at the beginning of the book that bears his

The Babylonian Captivity: Jews Into Exile

name. Imagine what it must have been like for Daniel: for the first 15 years of his life he enjoyed the comforts of his own home and family and then, suddenly, he was removed from the land of his youth never to return. For the student of the Bible many lessons of his fidelity to the LORD are revealed. Despite the loss of home and family, Daniel and his friends remained true to the LORD and in doing so have become examples to us today. Let us consider these "heroes in the fire."

1. Read Jeremiah 39:5-7. What insight do we gain about the cruelty of King Nebuchadnezzar?

2. Who was king of Judah when the Babylonians besieged the city of Jerusalem (Dan. 1:1-2)? Why did the Lord allow Babylon to defeat Judah and take captives? See 2 Kings 24:2-4.

TURNING POINT

The "turning point" in the life of Daniel and his friends Shadrach, Meshach, and Abednego is revealed for us in Daniel 1:2-3 where we are told Nebuchadnezzar brought them into the land of Shinar. Their lives would be forever changed because of their captivity in a foreign land, but some things would remain constant in their lives.

INSTRUCTIONS: Consider the verses below and indicate in each of the small boxes the five things that characterized Daniel and his friends (Hint: the key word in each begins with the letter "P.")

Daniel and his friends were young men of....

P _ _ _ _ _ _	**Daniel 1:8**

Why is this so critical to our walk of faith?

Relate this aspect of their character to Philippians 3:12-14.

P _ _ _ _ _ _ _ _	**Daniel 3:18**

Why is this so critical to our walk of faith?

Relate this aspect of their character to Genesis 39:9.

WHAT WOULD YOU DO FOR $10,000?

The percentage of Americans answering in the affirmative:

- Would abandon my entire family 25%
- Would abandon the church 25%
- Would become a prostitute 23%
- Would give up my American citizenship 16%
- Would kill a stranger 7%
- Would put my children up for adoption 3%

SOURCE: James Patterson and Peter Kim, *The Day America Told the Truth*, 1991.

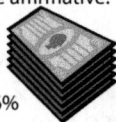

P_ _ _ _ _ _   **Daniel 6:4**

Why is this so critical to our walk of faith?

Relate this aspect of their character to Psalm 119:9-10.

P_ _ _ _ _ _   **Daniel 6:10**

Why is this so critical to our walk of faith?

Relate this aspect of their character to Proverbs 15:29, Romans 12:12.

P_ _ _ _ _ _ _ _ _ _ _   **Daniel 12:12**

Why is this so critical to our walk of faith?

Relate this aspect of their character to Psalm 130:5-6, Romans 5:3-5.

Nebuchadnezzar

Nebuchadnezzar was king of the Neo-Babylonian Empire, who reigned c. 605 BC – 562 BC. He conquered Judah and Jerusalem, and sent the Jews into exile. He is credited with the construction of the Hanging Gardens of Babylon and was the king who destroyed the temple in Jerusalem.

PURPOSEFUL LIVING

There can be no doubt that even at an early age Daniel and his friends lived purposeful lives. For them, even far from home and in captivity, they lived their lives for the LORD and devoted themselves to Him. These four young men can teach us a great deal about living in the 21st century. The key is to live with purpose. To know what our purpose is and to work daily to see that purpose accomplished. Of course, Daniel and his friends were not the only biblical characters who were purposeful in their living. Consider at least two additional examples:

What was Christ's purpose?

| |
| |
| *Luke 19:10* |

What was Paul's purpose?

| |
| |
| *Philippians 3:13-15* |

What about you? What is your purpose in life? Indicate below at least three goals that drive you to walk more closely to God:

| 1 |
| 2 |
| 3 |

BIBLE TURNING POINTS

I love to lose myself in the pages of a good book. This week I rediscovered a jewel of literature – an amazing and exciting book. In fact, I've read it several times because it is such a great story. The book is Esther. What makes the story so thrilling is that it is fact – not fiction, yet it reads like a novel. There is a heroine, a villian, intrigue, danger, and a happy ending. The story of Esther begins in the third year of Ahasuerus (Xerxes). During an extended feast Ahasuerus demanded his queen, Vashti, display her beauty before his drunken guests. When she refused, he deposed her in a burst of anger. A new queen was sought and the king chose Esther as the most beautiful and she was crowned the new queen. Soon after Esther's selection, Haman, a leading member of Ahasuerus' court, decided to kill all Jews because Mordecai – a Jew and the cousin of Esther – refused to bow down to him. In a fury, Haman persuaded Ahasuerus to sign a decree that all Jews should be destroyed. At the time Ahasuerus did not realize Esther was a Jew and that by agreeing to Haman's edict he was condemning her to death. Do a quick read of the book of Esther and then answer these background questions:

1. Why were there Jews still scattered throughout the Persian Empire given God's plans and desire? See Jeremiah 29:10-14.

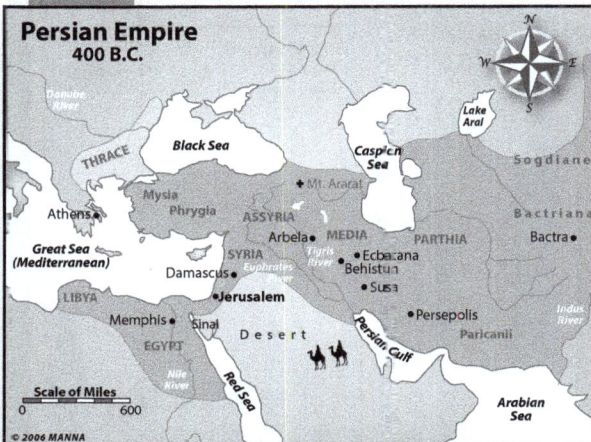

2. Why did Esther agree to be a candidate for queen?

3. How was Esther able to keep her lineage unknown given the stringent dietary rules for Jews?

4. How many times is God mentioned in the book of Esther?

5. Why was Esther chosen from amongst many other woman in the Persian Empire to be a part of the search for a new queen?

TURNING POINT

Esther 2:16-17: *Esther was taken to King Ahasuerus to his royal palace in the tenth month...in the seventh year of his reign. The king loved Esther more than all the women, and she found favor and kindness with him more than all the virgins, so he set the royal crown on her head and made her queen instead of Vashti.*

From Obscurity to Royalty

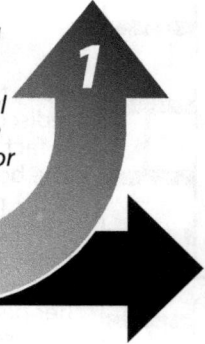

6. Why did Mordecai want Esther to keep quiet about her Jewish lineage (Esther 2:10)?

7. Was it wrong for Esther to keep silent about her origins and faith? Why or why not?

8. Why did Mordecai refuse to bow to Haman? Were Jews forbidden from bowing to others? See 2 Samuel 14:4; 18:28.

9. Why was Haman – the villain of our story – outraged that Mordecai refused to bow to him? See 1 Samuel 15:20-35.

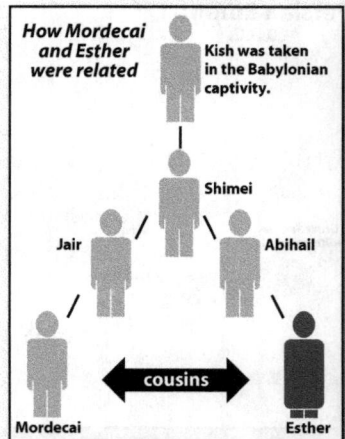

How Mordecai and Esther were related

Kish was taken in the Babylonian captivity.

Shimei

Jair

Abihail

Mordecai

cousins

Esther

TURNING POINT 2

Esther 4:14: *Do not imagine that you in the king's palace can escape any more than all the Jews. For if you remain silent at this time, relief and deliverance will arise for the Jews from another place and you and your father's house will perish. And who knows whether you have not attained royalty for such a time as this?"*

From Fearfulness to Fearlessness

10. What made Esther fearful about going to see King Ahasuerus?

11. Did the fate of God's people really depend on Esther? Why or why not?

12. Would it have been a sin for Esther to have kept silent? Why or why not? Consider Judges 5:23; Ecclesiastes 3:7, and James 4:17.

13. Write below what you believe to be the 2-3 most compelling lessons to be learned from the story of Esther. Be ready to share your observations.

Lessons we learn from Esther

Providence is, quite simply, the hand of God in the glove of history.

WE HAVE ATTAINED ROYALTY

Exodus 19:1-6 reads as follows:

Moses went up to God, and the Lord called to him from the mountain, saying, "Thus you shall say to the house of Jacob and tell the sons of Israel: 'You your-selves have seen what I did to the Egyptians, and how I bore you on eagles' wings, and brought you to Myself.
*Now then, if you will indeed obey My voice and keep My covenant, then you shall be My own possession among all the peoples, for all the earth is Mine; and you shall be to Me **a kingdom of priests and a holy nation**.' These are the words that you shall speak to the sons of Israel."*

14. As in our story of Esther, is there a death threat hanging over the heads of non-Christians? What is the death threat? See 1 Peter 5:8.

15. Like Esther, how are Christians described by Peter in 1 Peter 2:9?

16. Given the royalty we have achieved what is our responsibility?

Go ye into all the world, and preach the gospel to every creature.

Mark 16:15-16

12

BIBLE TURNING POINTS

TURNING POINTS

Our study of the "turning points" in the lives of men and women of the Bible is nearing completion. What we have studied reveals there are often times in our lives when we must make a critical decision, and in so doing, we may find ourselves on a new path leading in a new direction. Sometimes the "turning point" has immediate and obvious consequences. On other occasions the "turning point" does not reveal its significance until years later when we, in retrospect, see how that decision powerfully shaped our future and led us to where we are now.

"Turning point" decisions can be good or bad. They can lead us upward to a closer walk with the Lord, or downward into despair and spiritual death. Charles Kingsley (1819-1875), in a sermon he preached over a hundred years ago, put it this way: "...there comes a day of visitation, a crisis, or turning-point in our lives. A day when Christ sets before us, as he did for the Jews, good and evil, light and darkness, right and wrong, and says, 'Choose! Choose at once, and choose forever; for by what you choose this day, by that you must abide till death.'"

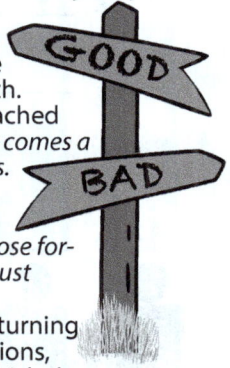

I have purposefully tried to focus on positive "turning points" in our study – that is, circumstances, decisions, and choices reached by both men and women which demonstrated their faith and fidelity to God. By way of review, we studied:

- **Abraham**, whose "turning point" obedience with Isaac proved his unshakable trust in God
- **Joseph**, whose "turning point" of bondage in Egypt revealed his immovable faith in God
- **Moses**, whose "turning point" was in accepting his role in leading God's people from Egypt
- **Joshua**, whose "turning point" was assuming the reigns of leadership and taking the promised land
- **Ruth**, whose "turning point" of selflessness ultimately brought her a glorious hope for the future
- **David**, whose "turning point" victory over Goliath revealed him as leader and future king
- **Elijah,** whose "turning point" was realizing he was never alone as long as God was with him
- **Jonah**, whose "turning point" came in learning of God's mercy for him and for everyone
- **Manasseh**, whose "turning point" of humility late in life led to his repentance and reform
- **Daniel**, whose "turning point" captivity revealed he was God's faithful servant even far from home
- **Esther**, whose "turning point" was in accepting she had attained royalty for God' purposes

OTHER BIBLE TURNING POINTS

There are many "turning point" moments in the lives of the men and women of the Bible. We have touched on but a few. Turning points can be in the circumstances and situations people confront, in the choices they are called upon to make, or in the responsibilities they are chosen to fulfill.

INSTRUCTIONS: In the spaces below, list at least five additional positive "turning point" examples in the lives of men and women of the Bible. Then, list five negative "turning point" examples.

Positive Turning Point Examples:

1 _____

2 _____

3 _____

4 _____

5 _____

Negative Turning Point Examples:

1 _____

2 _____

3 _____

4 _____

5 _____

TURNING POINTS IN YOUR LIFE

INSTRUCTIONS: Outline below one of the significant "turning point" events in your life. Turning points might be your conversion story or other significant events that put you on a path to a closer walk with God. If you are willing, be ready to share your turning point event with the rest of the class.

TAKING THE NARROW ROAD
The "Turning Point" to Salvation

A young Hindu student studying in the United States heard a speaker at a meeting say that Jesus Christ was the only Savior of the world. Afterward he said, "I do not like your idea that there is only one way to Heaven – your Christian way. I like to think that there are many ways – your way and mine, the way of the Christians, and the way of the Hindus, and the way of the Muslims and of all religions. Your way is too narrow. I like room on the road I travel. I want other people with me, not just my own group."

This all sounded very broad-minded. It was broad-minded. It was broad-road thinking. It leads to destruction. Not because the speaker said one thing and he said another; that is irrelevant. But Christ said one thing, and Hinduism says another. If Christ had said that men came to God through Hinduism, the young man could be right; but since Christ said, "No man cometh to the Father but by me" (John 14:6), the young man is dangerously wrong. He may want a broad road with room for all faiths. There is such a road indeed, but it does not lead where he wants to go. He must simply recognize the fact that there are but two roads, and they lead to different places. Until he learns it, until you learn it, you are on the broad road that leads to destruction. Jesus Christ ought to know because He is the author of salvation (Heb. 5:9).

In spite of the rigor of the narrow way so sharply in contrast to the ease of the broad road, this is a happy road. Christ *is* this road and Christ *is* the companion of this road. Those who bear His burden find that the burden is light, and those who are under His yoke find that His yoke is easy. Those who "lose" their lives discover that they really "find" them. Those who deny themselves, find themselves. Those who suffer while on this road are happy. This, in spite of all its hardships and demands is the glory road.

Source: From an article entitled "The Way: Straight and Narrow," by Dr. John H. Gerstner appearing online at www.the-highway.com

Then said Jesus unto his disciples, "If any man will come after me, let him deny himself, and take up his cross, and follow me." - Matt. 16:24

www.ingramcontent.com/pod-product-compliance
Lightning Source LLC
Chambersburg PA
CBHW071936020426
42331CB00010B/2894